WE LOVED YOU
EVEN BEFORE
YOU WERE BORN

Beatriz & Brian Thoele

love bug

To all the new little smiles and their adoring parents:

We created this book to be shared with your little one as you relive the magical moments before their arrival. We know how much they transformed your life even before they were born. Now, it's time to share your incredible journey with the very person responsible for it. We know that every pregnancy is different, but we hope that you at least had some of the same strange and wonderful experiences that we did. Enjoy!

Beatriz & Brian Thoele

When we found out you were coming, we were very happy. You were as tiny as a poppy seed, but you were big news!

A few weeks later, in the doctor's office, we could hear your heartbeat even though you were as small as a sweet pea.

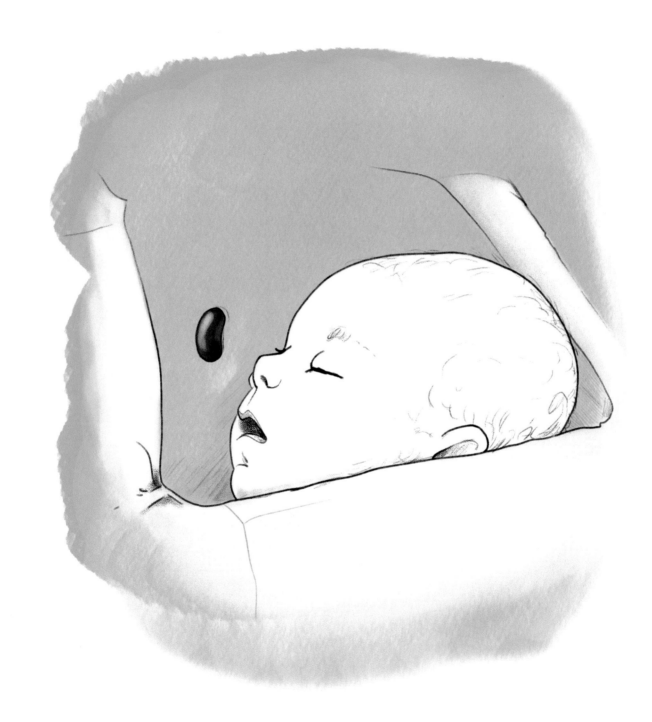

Mommy's stomach was feeling uneasy with all the changes. It was difficult, but that's also how we knew you were doing okay. You kept growing, and soon you were as big as a kidney bean.

One day, we found out if you were a boy or a girl. That was a big surprise! We couldn't wait to meet you! But you needed to grow more; you were only the size of a lemon.

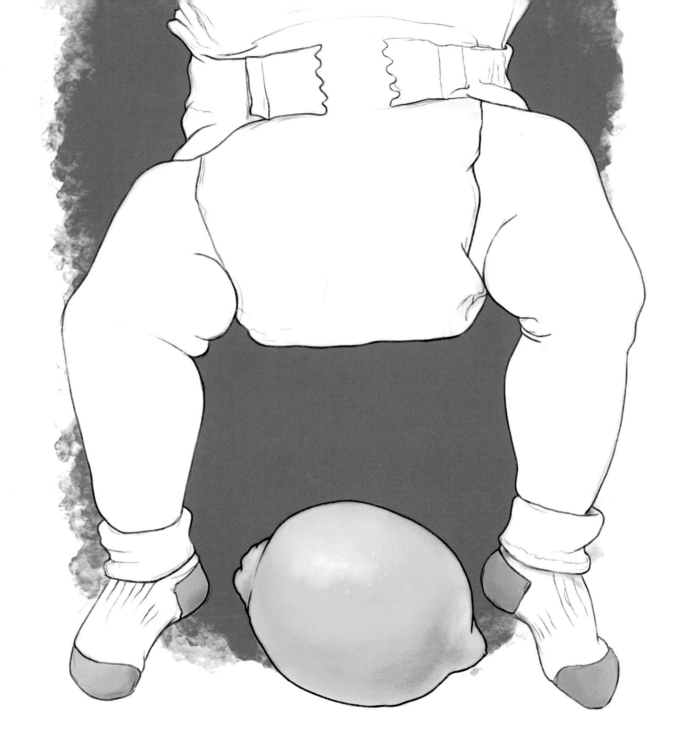

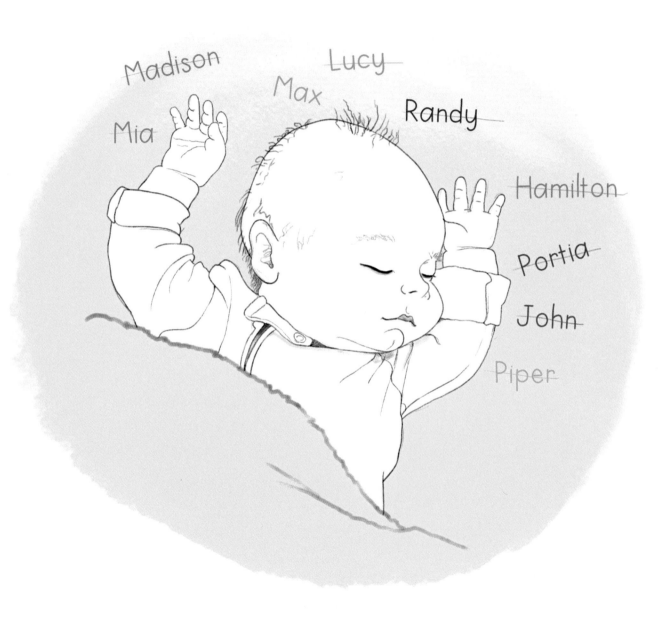

Madison

Lucy

Max

Mia

Randy

Hamilton

Portia

John

Piper

We started thinking of names, and eventually we came up with the perfect one for you.

We worried about lots of things. We read many baby books. We were already getting ready for you even when you were only as big as an avocado.

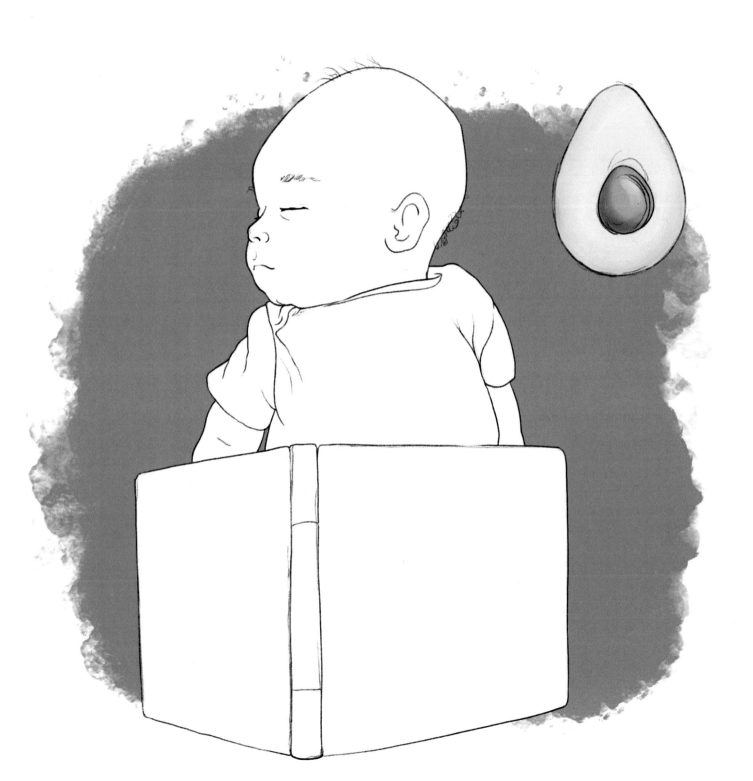

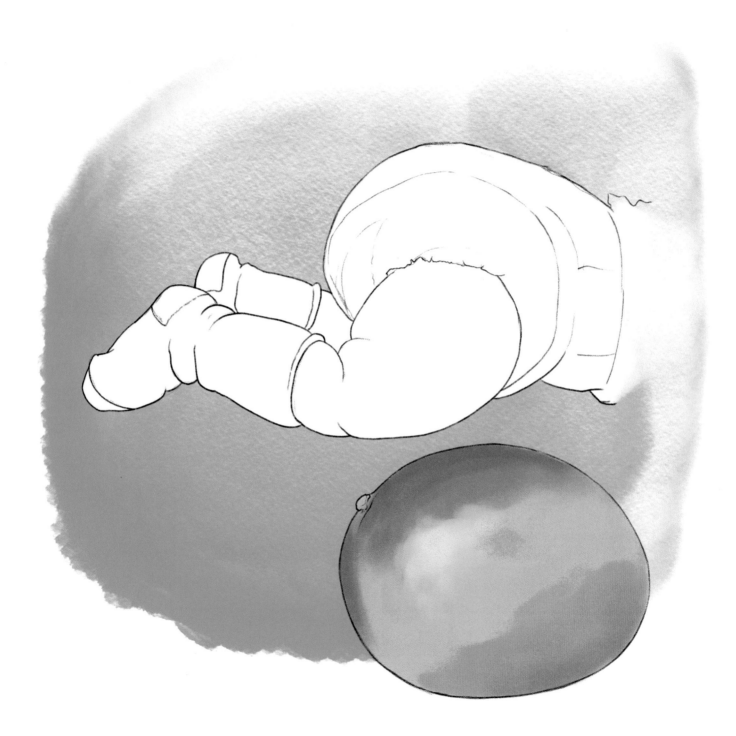

One night, mommy felt you kick for the first time! It was such a surprise that she gasped. You were constantly growing, but you still had a lot more growing to do because you were only as big as a mango.

Not so long later, we saw your adorable face using something incredible called an ultrasound. You looked very cute even though you were only about the length of a banana.

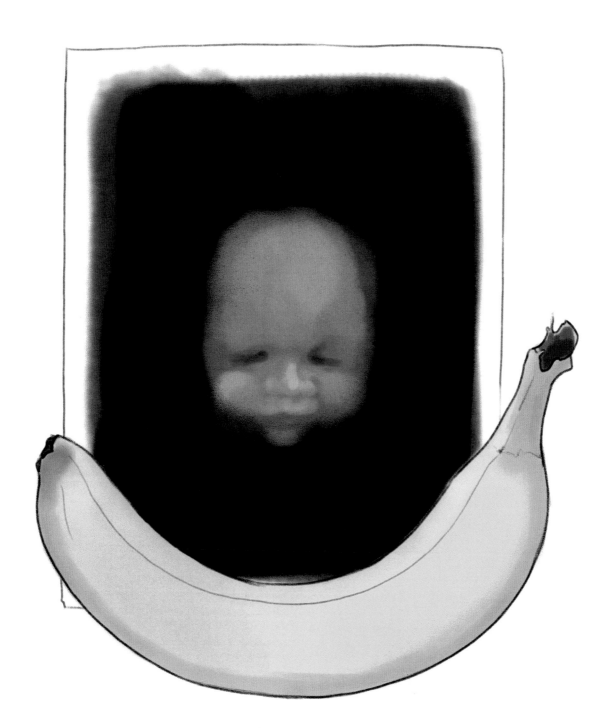

We started collecting all the things you might need—a stroller, a few toys, and even a tiny bathtub just for you.

Everyone was excited for your arrival. We received gifts from grandma and grandpa and many others. Before we knew it, you were as big as a cabbage.

You kept kicking. You were kicking so hard that we knew you would be strong. By then, you were as big as a cantaloupe.

We were impatient for your arrival, but you needed more time to get even stronger. While we waited, we packed a special suitcase to take to the hospital so we'd have all of our favorite baby clothes when you arrived. You were as big as a pumpkin!

When you were almost the size of a watermelon, you were BORN! We finally got to meet you!

We didn't know we were ready until you were here. You were even more special and wonderful than we had imagined.

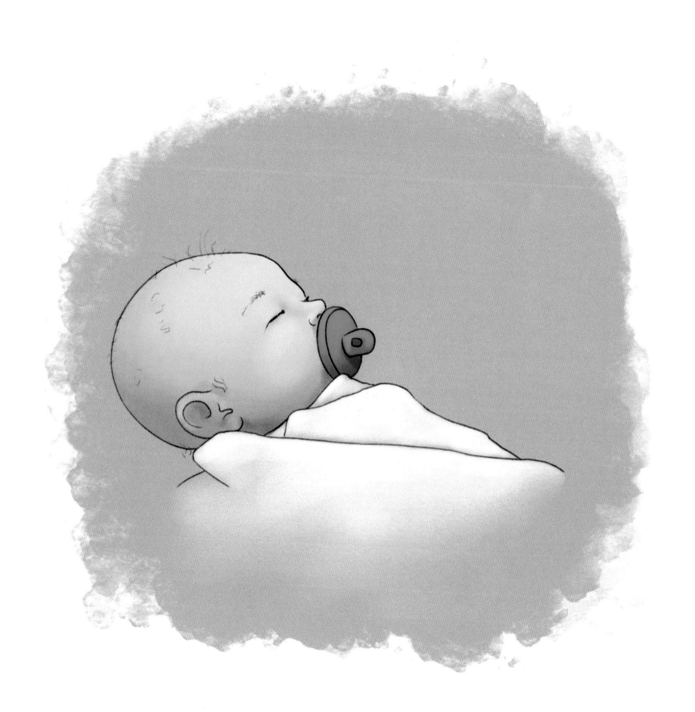

We felt like we already knew you. And even though we loved you before you were born, words can't describe how much we loved you when we finally held you in our arms.

THE END

Made in the USA
Middletown, DE
03 October 2024

61933985R00020